Straight Talk
About Death
with Young People

Straight Talk About Death with Young People

by Richard G. Watts

THE WESTMINSTER PRESS
PHILADELPHIA

PHOTO CREDITS: pp. 10, 16, 40, 54, Rohn Engh;
p.28, Joe Tritsch; p. 70, John Ellis.

BOOK DESIGN BY DOROTHY E. JONES

PUBLISHED BY THE WESTMINSTER PRESS®
PHILADELPHIA, PENNSYLVANIA

PRINTED IN THE UNITED STATES OF AMERICA

Library of Congress Cataloging in Publication Data

Watts, Richard G   1934–
    Straight talk about death with young people.

    Includes bibliographical references.
    1. Death—Juvenile literature. I. Title
BT825.W33   236'.1   75–12551
ISBN 0–664–24765–2

Contents

Preface 7

Introduction: *Straight Talk About Death* 11

1. *Growing Up with the Facts of Death* 17

2. *"What Is It Like to Die?"* 29

3. *Understanding Our Feelings of Grief* 41

4. *Why Do We Have Funerals?* 55

5. *Hopes People Live By—And Die By* 71

Notes 91

Preface

We live in a society that has many hang-ups, and the subject of death is one of them. We fear it. We try to avoid thinking or talking about it. We use many devices to hide from its reality. Yet death, as surely as birth, is a part of life. We must come to terms with it as we think through our faith.

Because adults so often have not come to terms with death, we try to protect our children from it. Yet I have found from working with seventh- and eighth-graders particularly that they appreciate open, honest, realistic discussion.

The more we learn about death, the better we can accept its inevitability. Irrational fear and dread tend to fall away once the subject is seriously examined. Openly talking about it tends to relieve anxiety. But more than this, as we learn we are better prepared to face it ourselves, and to be able to support and console others who are affected by it.

This book has grown out of my experience in working on the subject with young people of junior high age. Not being able to find useful resources for these discussions, I had to create my own. I invited a number of seventh- and eighth-grade students to meet with me to talk over the subject, to read over what I had written, and to share their own experiences in growing up with death.

Without their help, the book would never have been written. Because of their help, I offer it in confidence that it speaks especially to their interests and concerns. It is offered in the hope that an important gap in resources for young people will be filled, at least in part. It does not answer all questions, but it does seek to deal in a straightforward way with many that are significant.

Since the book represents the questions, the reflections, and the convictions of young people, I hope that many of them will read the book and reflect upon it. Parents, teachers, and youth leaders should find in it a starting place for honest discussion and serious dialogue with young people. I have found that when the subject of death is opened in church school classes or youth groups a lively response can be expected.

Now I want to say thank you to those young people whose contribution to this little book is so important. Thank you, Debbie Bouas, Mike Cunningham, Karen Davis, Beth Escott, John Friedhoff, Susan Green, Allen Greiner, Jim Hensey, Eric Hoffman, Mike Johnson, Suzy Mesdag, Beth Nobles, Mark Schildt, Cindy Schrantz, Tom Smith, Bret Swanson, Kathy Taylor, Fred Thomas, and Randy Young.

R. G. W.

Straight Talk
About Death
with Young People

Introduction

Straight Talk
About Death

Why do we need a book called "Straight Talk About Death"?

Death is a subject that most people have found very hard to talk about. In American society, death has for a long time been a taboo topic—something not to be mentioned in public.

Think of some of the ways in which we try to avoid the subject of death or deny its reality in our lives. If Grandmother dies, we beat around the bush with such phrases as "She passed away" or "She went to her reward." Even hospitals use words like "She expired." It is as though we were afraid simply to say, "She died." Perhaps if we do not use the word, death will somehow go away. We say that our pets are "put to sleep." We segregate old people into retirement communities or old people's homes, and so we need not be aware of their physical decline.

Just a hundred years ago, a boy or girl your age would almost surely have seen some members of the family die at home—would have watched breathing stop and color drain out of their faces. Nowadays few persons die at home with their families; most die out of sight in a hospital you may not even be allowed to visit. Of course we are grateful that modern medicine makes death less a constant threat than it used to be. In a country cemetery near my home, for instance, you can read heartbreaking stories written on tombstones—several children in a family swept away by death during a plague in the early 1800's. But the fact that we can grow up without encountering death makes us unprepared to meet it when, sooner or later, we must.

Another sign of our inability to face death is the custom of embalming bodies so as to make them appear lifelike. Still another is the trouble most people have talking with dying persons, helping them deal openly and honestly with their condition. In these and other ways we act like a society that is embarrassed and frightened by death, and therefore tries to pretend that it does not exist.

But this evasion causes problems. When we cover up our concern for any important part of human life, it comes back to haunt us in unhealthy ways of thinking. Take the subject of sex, for example. Back in the days (which still exist for some people) when sex was a subject no one was supposed to think or talk about, growing persons were often full of fears, worries, anxieties, misinformation, and wonderings about whether they were normal. Straight talk about sex helps to banish those worries and replaces a lot of silly myths with facts and healthy attitudes.

So also with death. Many people—children and grown-ups alike—have a lot of fears about death. Since the subject is not talked about openly, we find ourselves morbidly interested in news reports of murders, drownings, suicides, and other catastrophes. Maybe the conspiracy of silence about death helps to account for the intense interest that many people your age have in stories of ghosts, monsters, and murders. Death is a universal human concern. If we cannot talk about it openly, we will find other ways to satisfy our curiosity and handle our fears.

I have learned that many persons are eager for a chance to engage in straight talk about death.

About four years ago I began a study of death, funerals, and beliefs about life after death. I found the whole subject significant and interesting. So I began to lead classes of adults in the church on the theme "Death and the Christian Funeral." When a group got together, it seemed that I hardly had a chance to clear my throat before they jumped both feet first into the discussion. They seemed to have a lot to get off their chests. Some were angry about funerals that left them cold. Some thought it was a shame the way we keep old people alive artificially, with machines and tubes and transfusions, instead of letting them die peacefully and with dignity. Others were not sure what they believed about life after death. They often seemed relieved to have an excuse to talk about death with other people, to get out in the open the feelings they had bottled up inside themselves for so long.

Later, I began also to talk about the subject of death with junior high school students. To open up the subject, a group of adult leaders went on an overnight retreat with about fifty seventh- and eighth-graders. At one point, I asked the junior highs to write down any questions they might have and put them in a box. They came up with sixty-five different questions. Here are just a few of them:

What is the purpose of trying to preserve a dead body when it will decay sooner or later?
Why are there funerals? They only make people upset.

When do our spirits rise to heaven?

Is there a hell?

Should I grieve when someone dies, or should I do just whatever comes naturally?

Where do people get the impression that hell is hot and the devil is red, has horns and a tail?

Is death God's way of controlling overpopulation?

Can a dead person talk with someone who is living?

Perhaps you have had some questions like these in your mind too.

After talking with the youth group about these concerns, I became curious. I went over to the state university library to see what had been written for young people about death. I found almost nothing. There were books about young people and sex, religion, health, growth, dating, personality, family problems, vocations, and even distribution of their body fat—but nothing to help them understand death. And that's how this book began. I saw a need and felt a desire to help fill that gap. All the questions listed above—and many more—will be dealt with in these pages. You will not find here all the answers. But this book will give you some ideas to think about as you try to figure things out for yourself.

And now—let's have some straight talk about death.

Chapter 1

Chapter 1

Growing Up with the Facts of Death

You may find that you think more about death now than you used to. But probably the subject has been simmering on a back burner of your mind for many years. The new ideas that will come to you as a teen-ager do not just drop out of the blue, but emerge from a long process of experiencing, wondering, asking. Certainly this is true of your ideas of death. Our education in the "facts of death" as well as the "facts of life" begins a lot earlier than most adults realize. So in this chapter I will be inviting you to think about what has happened in your own growing up with the facts of death.

When did I first become aware of death?

Think back a moment to your own childhood. Can you remember when you first became aware of death? Can you remember how you felt about it? Maybe you can recall the time a pet died, how you felt, and what you wondered. You began to be aware of what made dead things different from living things: they could not move, or eat, or bark, or play anymore. You may have cried, and wanted your pet back. Maybe you and your friends held a "funeral" in the back yard for a gerbil or a goldfish or a rabbit. Perhaps your grandfather died, and you wondered where he went after dying. You may be able to recall some fears, perhaps associated with being alone, or in the dark, or worried about robbers coming to get you. Maybe at a time of a death in the family you felt left out and confused as adults tried to shield you from their own emotions. Whatever memories you may have, you can see that your education in the facts of death began rather early.

What were my first ideas of death?

Before I ask you to think about that question, let me throw in a word of caution. Much remains to be learned about how we develop in our understanding of death. It is a subject that has not received much attention. We do know, though, that we do not all develop according to the same timetable. You can readily see that in your classes at school. There are boys with high-pitched voices who have not started to shoot up yet, and tall boys with broad shoulders and husky voices and beginning beards. Both groups are normal—they just have different personal timetables for maturing. In the same way, we grow up emotionally and intellectually at different rates. So not everyone thinks about death in the same way.

Also, the kind of home background we come from has much to do with our dawning ideas of death. If your parents told you that at death "you take a ride on a star and go up to heaven," you will have a different attitude than if they simply said that "death is the end of a person's living, when he cannot share all the things we do anymore." But, with these cautions, we can say that probably you began your journey in understanding about death with ideas common to most children.

Probably before you started school you knew that death was a separation, but you did not believe it had to be complete or final. You thought that the person who died could be fixed or could come back. You certainly played some version of cowboys and Indians, in which you fell dead, and were very quiet, then jumped up again for the next game. Saturday-morning television cartoons probably reinforced this idea. No matter how badly Tom and Jerry were mangled by a wringer or bashed by a mallet, no matter how many times the hapless coyote plunged into the canyon chasing Roadrunner, they always miraculously returned to life for the next thrilling episode.

Besides thinking that death could be reversed, or undone, you may have believed that it did not ever have to happen to you. Death was something that happened only to very old people—and maybe by the time you got very old they would have found a way to make you live forever! Or you may even have decided never to grow up. Perhaps, too, as many children do, you connected death with violence, killing, or accidents—and worried about it.

But by the time you were nine or ten, you had learned that death is both universal and final. It happens to everyone, and it cannot be "fixed" or reversed. You began to understand it as one of the natural processes of life, which is part of the story of all living things.

So our ideas about death are set by the time we are ten or twelve?

Not at all! In fact, in some ways your growing up with death is just now beginning. You have learned that dying is part of a natural process by which all living things are governed. Now that you are past an early childhood stage of magical thinking, your reasoning powers are just coming into their own. You may do more thinking about what death means than you have ever done before. Here is how a group of seventh- and eighth-grade students responded to a statement in a survey I took:

	Agree	*Disagree*	*No Opinion*
I have more questions about life after death than I used to have.	45	11	15

Perhaps you also feel skeptical about some of the ideas you heard or were taught as a child. Later in the book, we will take a look at some of these ideas—heaven and hell, immortality and resurrection, and so forth.

In short, you are now beginning to fit the facts of death into a philosophy of life. You may be wondering, as one of my young friends put it: "Why are we all here on this planet, anyway? What's it all about?" You may have a sense of awe before the strangeness and mystery of the world as you grow into adulthood. Fitting death into the picture of life is one of the big jobs of adult thinking that you are now getting ready to tackle.

So I hope you will be patient with your questions and relaxed with your wonderings. It is good to think, to question, to wonder. And do not worry if you find yourself thinking about death quite often. It does not have to be a gloomy subject. Death is part of life, and the ability to think about death and ask what it means is part of the dignity of being human. The answers we come up with are an important part of what we call our philosophy or religion.

Where do our religious ideas about death come from?

One day I asked some of the young people who helped me write this book to take a pencil and paper and go to work on the subject "How My Ideas of Life After Death Have Changed." They expressed many different ideas. But most of them, when they were children, had fairly similar pictures in their minds. As I have mentioned, many thought that death was not permanent: "When I was little I thought that when you died you counted to twenty and jumped up again because that was the way you did it when I played."

Most of the group had also absorbed some ideas of heaven and hell. They thought of heaven in connection with fluffy white clouds, angels, and palaces. Their pictures of hell included fire, the devil, and pitchforks. Sometimes they thought of heaven and hell in terms of rewards for being good or punishment for being bad.

As we talked together about their childhood ideas, I asked whether they had got the angels, clouds, and palaces of heaven from Sunday school classes. To my surprise, they all answered in a chorus, "No!"

"Well, then," I went on, "where did the pictures come from? From your parents?"

Again the answer was "No."

So we began to talk. And it soon became apparent that the main source of their images of heaven had been television—especially Saturday-morning cartoons and a "special" called *The Littlest Angel.* In a cartoon like *Tom and Jerry* they sometimes watched a dead cat's "spirit" rise up like a ghost out of its body and go "up" to heaven where, presumably, it was blessed by warm milk, tuna fish, and lots of mice to chase! And from *The Littlest Angel* they got the clouds, the palaces, and even a factory for making angel wings. So it seemed that many supposedly "religious" ideas had not come from the faith of the church at all, but rather from the fantasies they had watched on television at an early age.

Of course, in some churches emphasis is placed on heaven and hell. And sometimes parents do try to comfort saddened children by saying that "God took Grandma to live with him." Such an idea may not endear God to the child, who would rather have Grandma *here.*

What are your own ideas about what happens to a person after death? Some young people, by the time they reach your age, have become skeptical about their childhood images of the "beyond." Some have begun to believe deeply that a person's spirit lives on after his body dies; and perhaps most admit to being confused when they try to make some sense out of the strange mixture of childhood fantasy, religious teaching, and scientific knowledge.

I thought you would be interested in reading what some seventh- and eighth-graders wrote about how their personal ideas about death, and life after death, changed as they were growing up. How would you write your own story?

BETH

My first ideas of life after death were fluffy white clouds where angels and Abraham Lincoln lived. I really couldn't be bothered about details. To me heaven was simply a place for angels and Lincoln—nothing less, nothing more.

My next recollection is when I said to my mother, "When you die and are in heaven you know what it's like but you can't tell anyone about it."

Now I suppose I believe that when you die your spirit simply stops. Most people that I know that have died had satisfying lives and there seemed no need for a life after death.

DEBBIE

1. My first thought of life after death was white angels, with gold halos above their heads. They lived above the clouds, right on top.

2. My second thought of life after death was when people died their spirits came back as ghosts (to get revenge).

3. My third thought of life after death was (and still is) when people come alive, after dying, only this time as another person, or animal.

KATHY

1. I always used to think that when you died and were buried, after a while your *whole body* went to heaven and you lived in heaven just like on earth but a lot better. Now I know that only your soul goes to heaven.

2. I thought that when you died someone always had to kill you and you could not just die naturally. I know now you can die naturally, somebody doesn't have to kill you.

3. I thought that if you were bad you would go to hell and the devil was waiting for you with a pitchfork

to stab and torture you. Now whether you are good or bad God forgives you and your soul still goes to heaven.

JIM

(3 to 6 years old) When I was a wee lad I thought the only people who died were grandmas and grandpas. And when they died they either went to heaven or to hell (most of them went to heaven).

(7 to 10 years) Every once in a while I would pick up a newspaper and I found out that other people die too. They don't have to be old—they can be any age, even my own!

(11 to the present) I began to get involved in the church, I shared my ideas with others, I formed new ideas. I became more critical on what the Bible said and now I have ideas I'm not sure of. Are they right? Should I believe what the Bible says about heaven?

SUSAN

At first I just thought that up in the clouds there was some kind of world (heaven) and I used to wonder what it was like (6 years).

Then I just sort of abandoned that idea the day we learned in science that clouds were water in a different form. I thought, Why would God want to live on water? But, as I had no new and exciting ideas, I was left out in the cold. When I got the idea about the clouds I thought that that was where you go in the end. My favorite game to play on long trips was to look up into the clouds and wonder what Grandpa was doing up there. I always thought about all the wings they must have to make.

That day in science class I was left bewildered, and I still am.

ERIC

At first when I was four or five years old I knew nothing of death. Then I started going to church and my thoughts changed from nothing into thinking there was a heaven and a hell. I stayed with this thought until it changed in the fifth or sixth grade. I started believing in heaven, hell, reincarnation, and life after death *all* together. I didn't know what to believe. Then when I came to Wednesday Club all the other thoughts went except life after death and reincarnation. I don't really know what life does exist after death, but whatever it is I'm certain it couldn't be heaven and hell because how could millions of people of the past fit in the sky? I believe they come back to earth as something else in reincarnation.

KAREN

Before, I thought after you died the only thing left was to go to heaven and fly around on clouds. Then all these other things have come up like being reincarnated, or just floating around as a spirit, or no life after death. There's no proof for any of them so I just wonder how we know which one to believe. How did people invent these different ideas—like what do they have to prove their idea was right?

When we went to a funeral for the first time I was surprised to see a body there because I thought right when you died you went to heaven. My buddies told me when you died God waited until after you were buried then took your body. Then I wondered why he left the bones after I saw pictures where they showed caskets with bones (skeletons). Then I learned about when bodies decay and wondered if God took anything or just left you there. I was very confused!

You can see that junior high years are, for many persons, a time of questioning, wondering, rethinking. For many years you just accepted what you were told—by parents, teachers, ministers. Now you are beginning to think many more questions through for yourself. That's as it should be. For only when you ask critical questions, such as, "Is that idea really true?" can you someday find it possible to say with conviction, "This is what I really believe!"

Chapter 2

Chapter 2

"What Is It Like to Die?"

Two hundred years ago almost every person who had lived as long as you have had watched someone die. It probably was a brother or a sister, a parent or a grandparent, and it usually happened at home. The death of a newborn baby was an accepted risk of childbirth, and it was actually unusual for a boy or girl to survive the first few years of life. In 1762 the French thinker and writer Rousseau, discussing the education of children, said:

> Of all the children who are born, scarcely one half reach adolescence, and it is very likely your pupil will not live to be a man.

A historian named Edward Gibbon tells us that his father kept naming all the boys Edward so that at least one of them would reach adulthood bearing the family name![1]

All that has changed, of course, and not many of us wish to go back to the "good old days." Vaccines, improved diet, better sanitation, modern medical and surgical skill, have brought us to a day when we simply assume that babies will

29

grow up, and when it seems a tragedy for any child to die. But add to this the fact that many old people die out of sight in a hospital or nursing home, and you have a new kind of society in which we may grow to maturity without ever seeing someone die. We have lost touch with the experience of natural death. The only deaths we are likely to see are those pictured in magazines and on television that are violent and tragic—assassinations, murders, deaths in battle.

The result is that we have fears and wonderings that we need to get talked out. For what was once an accepted part of life—death and dying—has now become, in its usual and natural forms, remote, strange, perhaps frightening. Adults turn quickly to news stories of wrecks, floods, murders, and other disasters, and young people are intrigued by ghosts, spirits, monsters, murders, and tales of the supernatural. Part of the reason for this is that we all need *some way* of dealing with our interest in, curiosity about, and fear of, death and dying. We are all in some way like the boy who wrote this letter to God:

Dear God
    What is it like when you die. Nobody will tell me. I just want to know. I don't want to do it.

Mike[2]

What is dying like?

In one sense, of course, what dying is like depends on many different things: whether death is sudden or comes at the end of illness, whether the dying person is young or old, whether he is a confident or a fearful person, and so on. On the other hand, some doctors and hospital chaplains who work day in and day out with dying persons have shared with us some of their insights, so that we can have an idea of what dying really is like.

One of these doctors is Elisabeth Kübler-Ross, who wrote a very helpful book called *On Death and Dying*.[3] For a number of years she has led meetings in which dying patients at Billings Hospital in Chicago have told doctors, nurses, and ministers what it is like, so that they might be of more help to others.

Dr. Ross says that those who are dying over a period of time from a terminal disease (rather than suddenly and without warning) often go through five stages in their reactions.

First, they react by denying that they are really going to die. They think, "Oh, no, not me—it can't be true." The shock of the news takes a while to wear off, but very few patients keep up the denial to the very end.

Second, they become angry. This is a natural reaction when they begin to realize that they are going to lose everything. The question comes up, "But why me?" They may take out their anger on members of the family, the hospital staff, or even God.

Third, dying people, says Dr. Ross, may bargain. Maybe in their prayers they promise God that they will do this or that if only he will let them live—perhaps until a wedding, or the birth of a baby, or the completion of a task.

Fourth, they become depressed. They are getting ready to let go of everything that has been important to them. At this time, family and friends should not try to "cheer them up," but just be with them and let them know that they are not alone.

Fifth, dying people often reach a stage of acceptance. Most of them die without fear or despair. Usually they have detached themselves from the concerns of life, and often, especially in old age or after long illness, are ready to accept death as a great relief.

Is dying painful?

This is a common question of young people, who often have exaggerated ideas about how much suffering is involved in dying. Illness may involve pain, of course, but modern medicines make it possible to keep most patients comfortable. Many embroidered tales of "death agonies" have been spread about, but often dying persons have a decrease in consciousness, and for the last six to twenty-four hours of life are entirely unconscious. Breathing may become very shallow, and gradually life just ebbs away.

One of the issues that you will find increasingly discussed in days ahead is "dying with dignity." Modern medicine, with its respirators, heart-lung machines, intravenous feedings, and other paraphernalia, is able to keep persons alive long after they would have died on their own. More and more people are rebelling against the idea of being kept alive as a "vegetable" instead of being allowed to die in a dignified manner. As one doctor concerned with this issue has put it:

Some day when I myself lie dying, I hope that I will have nearby some wise and kindly physician who will keep interns from pulling me up to examine my chest, or constantly puncturing my veins, or putting a tube down my nose, or giving me enemas and drastic medicines. I am sure that at the end I will very much want to be alone.[4]

Do dying people know that they are dying? Should they be told?

For a long time there have been arguments about whether to tell the truth to persons who are dying. Researchers such as Dr. Ross have found that doctors and nurses often refused to help them find dying patients to talk to on the grounds that such conversation would upset or depress them. But such worries really told more about the fears of the doctors and nurses than about the real feelings of the patients. While about four out of five doctors feel that a patient should not be told that he has a fatal condition, about four out of five *patients* say they *want* to be told! Typical responses are: "It is my life—I have a right to know," or "I don't want to be denied the experience of realizing that I am dying." In one way or another, dying people come to realize the truth, and they are only frustrated, usually, by the games of "let's pretend" that those around them feel they have to play.[5]

Perhaps we may say that dying people are not so much afraid of death as they are of being left alone, isolated, not loved and cared for. Telling patients about the seriousness of their condition should always be done with gentleness and with hope. But families that can talk and laugh and cry together, instead of keeping a stiff upper lip and pretending to one another, will be able to face death and grief with some measure of acceptance, and even of joy. The worst thing we can experience is not death, but being cut off from warm, open, and loving sharing with the persons who matter most to us.

What happens to the body after death?

You have perhaps heard tales of persons who were thought to be dead, but later turned out to be alive. Many such stories come from days before modern medicine, when precise ways of determining death were lacking. Doctors used to hold a feather before a dying person's nose to see if there was any breathing, or a mirror to his mouth, which would fog up if he still had breath. In a very good book called *Life and Death* (I think that every family should own a copy!), Herbert Zim and Sonia Bleeker tell how death is determined nowadays.

> Committees of doctors have agreed on tests for death. The person does not respond by sound or movement to anything painful such as a pinprick or a hard pinch. There is no reaction to heat or cold. When a strong light is pointed into the eye, the pupil does not contract. No muscle moves. If breathing is aided by a machine, the person does not breathe when the machine is turned off.
>
> Doctors tap arms and legs to test reflex responses. Upon death, reflexes stop and the tapping brings no response. Nor does the body respond with actions that we do without thinking, like yawning, blinking, or swallowing.
>
> All of these failures to react point out that nerves are not carrying messages to and from the brain. Thus, a final test for death is the failure of the brain to respond —"brain death."[6]

Ordinarily we still assume that death comes with the stopping of the heartbeat. However, with the development of machines that can keep the heart beating, *brain death* is becoming an important factor in determining when a person cannot be restored to life. This is also related to the increase in organ transplants. If brain death has occurred, doctors may feel able to remove organs quickly for transplanting even if a machine might still keep the heart beating.

For a description of the changes that take place in the dead body, let me refer again to Zim and Bleeker:

> After death, a person's temperature drops rapidly. The skin feels cold to the touch. The blood, which no longer circulates, settles and may appear as bluish patches under the skin. After several hours the muscles of a dead person contract, and the body becomes stiff. This condition is called *rigor mortis.* Later the dead muscles relax, and the body becomes limp again.[7]

Eventually, of course, bodily tissues disintegrate entirely, and where burial is the custom, the elements of the body decompose into the earth.

Why are people afraid of death and dying?

No doubt at some time each one of us has fears about death, fears that often are made more scary by our unwillingness to share them with others.

There is some reason to believe that younger persons are more fearful of death than older persons, and some fears are especially strong in childhood. Certainly one element is simply *fear of the unknown*—like walking into the dark. Childhood fear of death often includes *fear of being killed,* such as by a robber breaking into the house at nighttime. The *fear of the punishment of hell,* it is hoped, is less common than it used to be, but some churches and parents still threaten children with hell as punishment for being "bad." One of the greatest American pastors, Washington Gladden, who did a lot to apply Christianity to social problems around 1900, told how as a boy the fear of hell was always haunting him: "My most horrible dreams were of that place of torment." He used to lie in bed at night looking up in the grip of fright toward the stars, and it was not till age eighteen that a sensible minister taught him just to trust the love of God and do his best, confident of God's friendship.[8] We have already mentioned the *fear of the pain of dying,* which the young often exaggerate.

We may well wonder how many children fear their own death but do not admit it to others. One college-age girl said to me: "When I was tiny, I would often lie in bed crying at night, thinking of what it would someday be like to die: *me,* die and be put in the ground and be covered with dirt, never to see any of the world again. This is not the type of subject that one talks about with friends all the time, and I've never been exposed to it at home."

Another childhood fear is of *being the cause* of someone's death. We will consider that in the next chapter.

While some of our fears are groundless (like those of teen-agers who, upon becoming aware of death, worry over little aches and pains, fearing that they are signs of some dread disease), some of our fears are reasonable ones. To be afraid of our own death—or at least not to accept it gracefully—is just normal. Life is a wonderful gift, and to think of being cut off from sun and sky and stars, laughter and play and work, is enough to send a chill into any person's heart.

But perhaps hardest of all is to accept death as cutting us off from those we love. I find that many persons fear the death of those they love more than their own death. To be bereaved seems worse than to die. And it may be hard indeed to think of the grief and loneliness of those left without us when we die. Human death is peculiarly grievous and shocking because human beings have the ability to love. The only way not to hurt is never to love—and that would be worse than having to face death.

How can we handle our fears about death?

First, we can bring those fears out into the open and talk about them. If you have any such fears that trouble you, find a person you respect and trust, and share them. Fears kept inside and brooded about just grow bigger and scarier; fears that are brought out into the light of day and shared often vanish like bad dreams at daybreak. At least they are easier to deal with.

Secondly, we can realize that death is, after all, a part of all life. A dog may live for fifteen years, a horse for thirty, and a man for seventy-five, but all living creatures eventually die. In this way, change and variety is possible for life, and younger generations have their chance at seeing what they can make of the world.

Thirdly, we can let the fact of death inspire us to make the most of our life. It is a strange thing that often persons only begin to savor their life and fully enjoy it when they have a brush with death. I remember talking once with a man who had recovered from a nearly fatal heart attack. He said something like this to me: "You know, I just sit out in the yard now and I notice the blue of the sky and the green of the grass, and I watch the birds. Now everything is a miracle!" By facing death, he was inspired to treasure life.

Chapter 3

Chapter 3

Understanding Our
Feelings of Grief

Sooner or later, death comes so near to us that it deeply affects us personally. When someone who is very close to us dies, death becomes much more than a matter of facts and speculations. We experience many different kinds of feelings—disbelief, sadness, fear, anger, regret—feelings that are all part of the emotional reaction we call *grief.* Often our grief feelings are so strong that if we do not understand what is happening to us, we may be unable to cope with them. So now we want to take a look at our grief feelings and try to understand them better.

Do all people feel grief in the same way?

In a word: No.

How we feel when someone dies depends upon many things. First, it depends upon who the person is to us. We are not likely to feel as strongly about the death of a cousin in another state, for example, as we do about the death of a brother or a sister. We may or may not be upset by a grandparent's death. One boy whose grandfather died said, "I didn't really feel anything—I kind of felt sorry for my mom."

Second, how we feel depends upon the circumstances of death. The death of an old person who has been helpless and "out of touch" for years in a nursing home may produce feelings of thankfulness and relief, whereas the accidental, sudden death of a child or person in "the prime of life" may leave us feeling shocked and angry.

Third, our way of grieving depends also upon the kinds of persons we are, whether we express our feelings easily and openly or tend to keep things inside. All these factors add up to this: There is no one "right way" to feel grief.

What does age have to do with grieving?

Another aspect of grief may be of interest: It seems that persons may grieve in different ways at different stages of life.

Children have a tendency to express grief in their way of behaving. Perhaps the reason is that they have not yet learned to understand their inner feelings or to express them very well to other people, and so tend to "act them out" instead.

Adults are more likely to express grief through emotional responses. They do more crying, more anguished talking; their sadness and loneliness and bewilderment are more obvious to other persons around them.

Older people apparently often grieve physically. Their mourning may take a toll on their health, so that symptoms of bodily distress crop up more commonly in bereavement than is true for other groups.

All these ways of grieving may be found, however,

among persons no matter what their age; physical symptoms, emotional expression, and "acting out" may all be part of our response to the death of someone we love.

What do you mean by saying that children tend to act out their grief?

To a young child, death means being left alone. Children are almost totally dependent upon their parents, and the death of one of them, especially the mother, brings their whole world crashing down around their heads. In what may appear to be strange behavior to adults, bereaved children may go about their play almost as if nothing had happened. An adult may say, "My, isn't Johnny taking it like a brave little man!" It is more likely, though, that Johnny's loss is so devastating to him that he will not admit its reality, and in his play is keeping life "as usual" until the parent returns. Johnny may be too immature to know how to express his feelings to those adults who think he is acting bravely.

One school psychologist, working with bereaved children, says that while six- to nine-year-olds may be able to admit that they are unhappy, nine- to twelve-year-olds hardly ever are able to do so. But their bottled-up grief has to be expressed somehow. So such children who have lost a parent will often begin to do badly in their schoolwork, may daydream more than usual, may stay away from friends, or may stick closer to home than usual. These ways of behaving show the grief that is inside, which the youngster does not know how to get out.

Teen-agers also may act out their grief. Recently, a study was made of 14 persons between the ages of fourteen and seventeen who were under the wing of the California Juvenile Probation Department for delinquent behavior. In every case this behavior which got them into trouble followed the death of a close family member. Since all the boys and girls involved had formerly behaved in acceptable ways, their "bad" behavior seemed to be a way of getting out the grief that they did not know how to express otherwise. Perhaps included in their grief was anger, and perhaps a sense of guilt which made them want to do something that would bring punishment upon them.

To these kinds of grief responses we need to turn now.

What feelings enter into children's experiences of grief?

Many confused, mixed-up feelings come over us when someone close to us dies. A wise and understanding rabbi, Earl Grollman, who has worked with many bereaved children, has listed for us some of these feelings which are part of the experience of grief.[9]

1. *Shock and denial.* The shock of a nearby death may be so great that we just can't accept it. The child may say: "I don't believe it. It didn't happen. It is just a dream. Daddy will come back. He will! He will!"

2. *Physical problems.* Grief may show up in complaints of physical symptoms: "I don't want to eat—I'm not hungry at all"; "I can't sleep"; "I had a nightmare."

3. *Anger.* When we are young, we see the people around us as important to satisfying our own needs and keeping us safe. If a parent dies, we may feel rejected and abandoned. We ask, "Why did Daddy (or Mother) do this to me?" We may also direct anger elsewhere: toward the doctor for not making Daddy well, toward God if God is thought of as "taking" people away to be with him, or toward the minister. One child blurted out, "The minister doesn't know any-

thing—he keeps saying God is good."

4. *Guilt.* Whenever someone dies, one of our first reactions is to think of all the wrong things we thought, or said, or did toward that person—or all the good things we failed to do. We may suddenly realize that there is no longer any way to "make up." Young children may even feel that they were in some way responsible for the death because of their bad thoughts, words, or deeds. This is such an important point that I want to return to it in just a moment.

5. *Other reactions.* Other possible reactions that express grief include: (a) trying to find another person (Uncle Ben) to replace the lost parent; (b) trying to talk or walk or act like the deceased person, as if taking his place in the family; (c) exaggerating the good qualities of the person who died; (d) believing that we are suffering physical symptoms like those of the person who died; (e) feeling panic at the idea that perhaps soon no one will be left to care for us.

Why do we feel guilty
when someone close to us dies?

Sometimes a child will feel that he is in some way responsible for the death of someone close. He feels guilty. It is important for us to understand the reason for this feeling.

Very young children cannot distinguish between a *wish* and a *deed.* They tend to think in a magical way, believing that thoughts and wishes are able to make good or bad things happen in the real world. This sometimes causes them a great deal of worry when a person they love dies. (Adults sometimes return to this magical thinking in the shock that follows a death; they also may feel somehow responsible.)

Our life with other people is always a mixture of feelings —love and anger, thankfulness and resentment. Every normal child gets terribly angry with his parents from time to time, and wishes they would leave, or die—the child may even yell at his mother, "I wish you were dead!" (One six-year-old said to his mother: "I wish you had never been alive! And then other times I don't feel like that at all. Are you like that with your mother?")[10] You can see that if Mother really did die, the child might suppose that it happened because he wished it to be so. Because he is used to being punished for being bad, it is easy for him to think of the death as a punishment for his "bad" thoughts.

Here are a few real-life examples of this magical thinking of childhood.

One six-year-old said: "I should have given Tim my tricycle. He wanted it, Mummy. Then he wouldn't have died, would he?"

"Is it my fault that Granny died?" an eight-year-old girl asked. "I didn't carry her bags up the steps."[11]

Because most of us do not understand these feelings as we are growing up, we may be plagued by them into adult life. Once I talked with a college student who was quite upset about the whole subject of death. It happened that when she was six years old her grandfather died. Just a few days before that sudden death, her grandfather had wanted to take her to the movies, but the girl, busy playing with her friends, refused to go. When her grandfather died, she felt terribly guilty for not doing what her grandfather wanted. Even as a young woman the memory still haunted her.

Another woman tells how, when she was nine, her father died after a long illness. She was always being told that "Daddy isn't expected to live through the night," and in many ways she hated him for not dying, because she was somehow held responsible: "Be quiet, your father can't rest if you make so much noise." When her father did die, she believed that it was because she had wished it so. Years later, she still would not form close relationships with other persons because she felt she would lose them through death, for which she would be responsible.[12]

Sometimes we find ways to "make up" for the bad wish that we are afraid caused a death. One small boy's pet dog was killed by an automobile. At first he was shocked, and then he blamed it on his parents for not taking good enough care of the pet. But really he was angry with himself, because he had once expressed the wish to be rid of "that awful pest." When a burial service was held for the pet, the boy insisted on burying one of his favorite toys with it. This was a sort of "peace offering" that quieted his conscience, which was feeling uneasy over the "bad" wish.[13]

Are these various grief reactions normal?

This is a very important question. One of the big problems of grief is that we experience many confused and troubling feelings that are new to us. We may be very upset if we feel angry with the dead person, because that is not the emotion we want to feel. Or we may wonder if we will ever be able to eat or sleep right again. And it certainly is disturbing to wonder if our angry wishes are somehow responsible for illness and death. Sometimes grieving people feel that their minds are "running away" with them, that they are "cracking up." That is why it is so important to know that *all these reactions and feelings are natural.* They are, by the way, just as common among adults as they are among children. In fact, death is so hard for many adults to handle that they sometimes revert to the fears and fantasies of childhood. There is cause for concern only when these feelings persist over a long period of time and do not go away or lessen.

Usually, they pass with time—and they will fade faster if we realize that they are quite normal and if we do not worry about them unnecessarily.

As far as children are concerned, we need especially to reassure them that, in Mister Rogers' understanding words, "scary, mad wishes don't make things come true." All of us are angry at times, and all of us have hostile thoughts and wishes. This is just a normal part of our living together. If we can accept the angry thoughts without worrying too much about them, we will find that the loving, warm memories come flooding back into consciousness. For in our families there is also much mutual caring, helping, loving. Not even death can take these good memories away from us.

How can we get over our times of grief?

We have already been talking about one of the important ingredients in a healthy response to grief: recognizing that our various feelings are normal, and that with time we will move beyond most of them.

Another thing we can do to help is simply to *express* our grief, to get it out in the open. Bottled-up feelings just build up pressure till they pop the cork. It is hard for many of us to seek out another person and say: "Will you listen to me? I'm feeling unhappy"—or frightened, or worried, or angry. It is especially hard when the feelings we need to express are negative ones, feelings that are not socially approved. But by talking things out with someone we trust, we can often solve in two days problems that we might otherwise brood about for months.

Another aspect of expressing grief that we should say a word about is *crying*. In our society, from about age three, when little boys stub a toe or fall from a tricycle, they are constantly told, "Now, now, big boys don't cry." Then when they are thirteen or thirty and need to cry, they don't know how. This restriction on crying is not only silly but also dangerous. Tears are one way God gives us to express the love we have for the person who has died. They are also one way God gives us to release the inner pressure of grief— pressure that can hurt us if it is not released. A family crying together in shared grief is beautiful. It is nothing at all to be ashamed of.

One more thing. As we move through grief, more and more we invest our love and caring in other people. No matter how great a loss we have suffered, there are others who will love us and who need our love. We honor the memory of those we love, not by staying fixed back where we were with them, but by moving ahead to share with others the love we learned from them. It is by returning to the unfinished business of living that we find fresh hope and gladness.

How can we be helpful to friends who are grieving?

First of all, let's talk about how *not* to help. Usually, grieving persons are not helped by others who offer them explanations (including religious explanations) of why the death happened. Sometimes well-meaning friends talk about how it was the will of God that an accident or illness occurred. Apart from the fact that such persons are being rather presumptuous in pretending to know so much about the will of God, such explanations rarely comfort anyone. Rather, they may provoke anger with God for doing such a thing. We do not think of God as pushing buttons to make people live or die. Death is a part of God's overall ordering of his creation, not a punishment that he metes out whenever he gets the notion.

Secondly, it is perhaps most helpful just to "be with" your friend. Often when we hear of a death we feel miserable and helpless. We wonder, "What can I say?" Frequently the answer is, "Nothing—nothing at all." But people do not need our words as much as they need *us,* our presence, our concern, our listening, our friendship, our reassurance that they will not be left alone in their grief.

Thirdly, we can help grieving persons keep alive the memory of their loved ones. I remember talking one time with a widow whose husband had died after fifty-two years of marriage. She said to me, "My friends come by and they say, 'Maude, with time you'll forget.' " Forget! No one ever forgets, or should forget, half a century of devoted life together. It is our task as friends to help such a person remember, by sharing reminiscences, by speaking freely of the deceased person, by keeping alive what he has meant to her. I like the way the Bible speaks of our need to "rejoice with those who rejoice, and weep with those who weep."

Finally, a suggestion that is as vital as it is simple. To help a grieving friend, take time for him or her after the funeral is over. It often happens that in the interval between death and the funeral, a person is flooded with expressions of concern and with a hubbub of activity. But once the funeral is over, friends and relatives go back to their own jobs and families, leaving the grieving person very much alone. Yet this is apt to be just the time when, as the first shock of loss wears off, that person faces the full sorrow, loneliness, and depression that are part of grief. Just at the point when the formal rituals end, the time for continuing friendship and support really begins.

And a closing story

A few weeks ago I talked about death and grief in our church, and then invited the people to share their thoughts and experiences in response. The next week I received a long letter from one elderly lady, telling me some of the things she would have said if her voice were stronger. One part of her letter told of the warm and understanding way her father helped her in a time of childhood grief.

I should also have liked to tell of how my father handled the question of death with me when a sister, several years older than I, died when I was almost six. He did not say she had gone to heaven nor that she was with Jesus. Instead, he held me in his arms and wept and then said: "Honey, Sister is dead and we won't ever see her anymore. It will be lonesome without her. You will miss her so much at bedtime, for she won't be here to get you ready for bed and tuck you in. She can't ever do that again and you will be lonesome and sad. All of us will miss her, for all of us loved her. Everybody has to die. Some die when they are old, but some die young, like Sister. It's too bad but that's the way it is. For a long time, all of us will feel like crying and sometimes we will cry. You can always come to me and cry whenever you feel like it. But finally, we'll all get used to living without her, and we'll stop crying, even though we'll *never* forget her."

The above is not my happiest memory of my father because it was very, very sad. Yet, it is one of my cherished memories, for, even though I was so young, I felt secure. I felt his great love, understanding, and compassion. Later, I realized he had been completely honest with a small child and that this was perhaps the main reason for my feeling of security. Perhaps the best thing of all was that he let me share his sorrow. We had wept together. I believe this kind of sharing was as unusual then as it is now—perhaps more so.

The death of someone close to us is a hard experience. But with this kind of honesty and sharing of emotions, we can help one another come through it strengthened and more mature.

Chapter 4

Chapter 4

Why Do We Have Funerals?

All human cultures that I know of hold some kind of special rites following a person's death. These rites may involve feasting or fasting, crying or dancing, faith or fear, but they all bear a common testimony that death is not a matter of indifference to any of us. All the great occasions of life— birth, coming of age, marriage, death—seem to call forth observances that mark them as times of special significance.

In the United States today, we are in the midst of a period when such rituals are out of favor. Many persons seem to view ceremonies, including sacred ceremonies, as a waste of time. American attitudes toward funeral customs in particular are beginning to undergo change. During the 1960's books began to appear that criticized expensive funeral customs, such as embalming, satin-lined caskets, and waterproof cemetery vaults. I find that many individuals are turned off also by such customs as viewing the dead at a "visitation."

Our problem seems to be this: At the time of death we have a need for some special observances, but the ones we have inherited often fail to help us. In this chapter we will make a few suggestions about how rituals at the time of death can be made more meaningful. But first, why are such observances necessary?

Why do we have funerals at all?

I will be using the word *funeral* in a broad sense, to refer not only to the worship service that occurs after someone dies but also to the related ceremonies and customs that go with it. And I think we can say that there are six main purposes of funeral rites—whatever those rites may be:
1. To mark the disposition of the body
2. To help people face the reality of death
3. To give family and friends a chance to express their grief
4. To honor the memory of the dead person
5. To renew community ties among the living
6. To put death in some kind of religious perspective.

What is the usual form of a funeral?

Although funeral customs vary greatly around the world, here in the United States about nine out of ten funerals follow a common pattern. The observances can be divided into three main parts.

First, there is a time of "visitation," or viewing, at a funeral home (which may also be called a mortuary or chapel). At the visitation the embalmed body is usually on display in an open casket, and the family is present to receive expressions of sympathy from friends who come by.

Second, usually the day after visitation, a service of worship is held, generally in the funeral home, although some religious groups (especially Roman Catholic, Episcopalian, and Lutheran) emphasize holding services in the church instead. The funeral service is led by a priest, rabbi, or minister, and consists of prayers, Bible readings, and sometimes a sermon or remembrance of the person who died.

Third, following the funeral the casket is carried in a hearse to the cemetery, where a committal service is held. This is usually a brief service of prayer, during which the body of the person is committed to the ground and his or her spirit to God. The actual lowering of the casket into the ground is ordinarily delayed until the mourners have left the cemetery.

So this is the typical funeral pattern: a public visitation, a public worship service, and a public committal.

Now let's take a look at how such observances relate to the six purposes of all funeral rites.

Main purposes of funeral rites

1. To mark the disposition of the body

Obviously, when a person dies, his or her body must be removed in some way. The dead body can no longer relate to us in any meaningful way, but since it was the outward form of a person we loved, we do not simply "throw it away," but treat it with respect. There are several alternative ways of disposing of dead bodies.

The most common method in our country today is to place the body in a casket or coffin and bury it in the ground, where eventually it will decompose. A less common method is cremation, in which both casket and body are burned, and the ashes either buried or stored. A building in which either ashes or bodies are kept above ground is called a *mauso-*

leum. A survey of some three thousand mostly younger Americans shows that there is a movement away from burial toward cremation and donation.

> If it were entirely up to you, how would you like to have your body disposed of after you have died?

Burial	22%
Cremation	31%
Donation to medical school or science	32%
I am indifferent.	16%

(This survey was conducted by *Psychology Today* magazine.)[14]

Concern for cremation may be related partly to a growing awareness that land used for cemeteries is growing scarce —particularly in urban areas. In England in 1963 the Cremation Society claimed that 41 percent of all bodies were cremated.

Recently more attention has been given to donating bodies to medical schools. Future doctors gain much of their knowledge of the human body through the dissection of specially preserved corpses, which are called cadavers. Forms are available by which people may bequeath their bodies to science in this way. For a long time, also, we have had eye banks, to which people might will their eyes so that others might see. With the increasing ability of surgeons to transplant such vital organs as kidneys and hearts, we may well see more and more such arrangements giving parts of bodies away after death, in order to be useful to others who need the organs for life.

2. To help people face the reality of death

In regard to grief, we said that our first response to a death is often one of shock, denial, and disbelief: "Oh, no—I just can't believe it!'' The shock of the loss is so great that we cannot realize that the loved person is actually dead. And so one of the purposes of rites at the time of death, extending over several days, is to help persons face death as a fact, so that eventually they will be able to readjust their lives to new realities.

Much of the debate that swirls around funerals these days focuses on whether or not our customs really do help people face up to death. Consider, for example, the common custom of viewing the body at a visitation.

Some argue that the practice is helpful because as family and friends see the lifeless body they have to accept the fact that death has really happened. On the other hand, it may be argued that the mortician's skill has made a dead body look so lifelike that it is much harder to realize that the person is dead. Most bodies are embalmed, a process of injecting chemical fluids into the body in order to preserve the tissues (for a time) and give the skin a lifelike tone. Also, morticians use various cosmetics to add color, as well as providing hairdos and dressing up the bodies in formal clothes. Some people argue that the end result is not the viewing of a dead body so much as of a body artificially doctored up to look alive, and perhaps temporarily sleeping. That may make it harder to see death for what it is—the end of life and the beginning of a process of dissolution of the body.

Not long ago I attended a funeral for a woman well over ninety years old. I had visited her many times in a hospital during her last illness. The day before she died, I saw her, spoke to her, and prayed with her. I remember that the years had chiseled deep furrows into her brow and cheeks. She looked very old, very weary—as indeed she was. Her memories went all the way back to rugged days of pioneer life.

When I saw her body laid out at the funeral, I was dismayed and angry. The mortician's skill had made her look twenty years younger. Her skin was smooth and unwrinkled. She was "pretty," not tired, old, and worn. Cosmetics had wiped away the hard-won etchings of the years, and erased the dignity of her death. I prefer to remember her lying in a hospital bed. Real dying has more meaning to it than pretended life.

No doubt there are times when it is a kindness to soften the marks of long suffering, and so leave the grieving with a happier image of their loved one. But surely we may say, of all funeral customs: if they cover up the reality of death, they are not helpful in the long run; if they assist the bereaved to cope with death realistically, they are. For until we see death as a real event, we cannot move beyond it to new life and fresh hope.

3. To give family and friends a chance to express their grief

One of the misconceptions many people have is that it is especially "Christian" to be strong, brave, and always composed while grieving. If a widow hides her deep sadness, and sheds no public tears, we tend to say, "My, isn't she taking it well!" But in the last chapter we saw that an important part of working our way through grief is first of all to *express* it. And meaningful funeral rites should give opportunity for such expression.

In days gone by, public expression of emotions at death was common. In our day, many persons feel embarrassed by such "display." Often at funeral services the grieving family is hidden from other worshipers in a separate room, as though it would be a shameful thing if friends and neighbors should catch them crying. Often friends do not know how to express their caring, and they avoid words or gestures like hugs and kisses that might provoke tears. Let's just say it plainly: it is all right to cry in public at a visitation or a funeral service.

A few years ago I went to a memorial service for a two-year-old daughter of a friend of mine. From birth she had had a rare bone disease, and finally died. Since the members of that particular church do not generally have strong beliefs in heaven, resurrection, or other traditional religious ideas, the service included instead some poems about nature and beauty, and some beautiful words from the minister. To me the whole service was boring and unhelpful. The poems did not find any responsive chord in me.

But there was one point at which God's love and goodness came through to me. That was when the little child's family walked into the church, and I saw that her mother was quietly crying. That was very real, and it moved me deeply. Sometimes the open expression of grief says better than words ever can how beautiful love is, and how hard it is to let go of someone who has loved us, and whom we have loved too.

4. To honor the memory of the dead person

Funerals do not simply help us come to terms with death, as an idea, but with the death of one particular person who matters to us. And so funerals should include memories and impressions of the one who died, as a way of honoring what that person has meant to us and what of his or her life we want to make a part of our own.

Not long ago an elderly lady died in our town. Before the funeral, I went over to her house, where her husband, her daughter, and her grandchildren were all together. Suddenly we found ourselves sharing good memories. Her husband was thankful for a devoted partner in marriage. Her daughter told me how, when she was a little girl, she remembered hungry men coming to the back door asking for food, and how her mother never turned a needy person away. The five grandchildren remembered days of Grandma playing the piano and singing with them. They broke out laughing when they recalled how she would give them all fishing poles to hang over the front porch, and then would put little surprises on the end of the line! Soon we were all laughing with shared gratitude for such warm memories. And many of these family memories became part of the funeral service the next day, for we wanted to honor the very unique and irreplaceable person who had died.

In recent decades, funerals have changed a lot in this matter of honoring the dead. In days gone by, funerals often included *obituaries* and *eulogies.* An obituary is an outline of a person's life that tells of some significant happenings— dates of birth, marriage, children, jobs held, and so forth. A eulogy is a speech praising the dead person. Well, it used to be that eulogies were often so flowery and exaggerated that you would suppose the dead person was a candidate for sainthood. The story is told about a widow who sat listening to the preacher go on and on about the glorious virtues of the deceased, till finally, unable to take it any longer, she tiptoed over to the casket to see if it was really her husband! In reaction against flowery eulogies, many ministers have moved to what one of my friends calls the "anonymous funeral"—you know that somebody has died, but from the service you would never be able to figure out who. One recent study showed that a large group of ministers never even referred to the dead person in any way in well over half of their funeral services.

It seems to me that we should be able to avoid both extremes—of either praising the dead to the high heavens or ignoring their life altogether. Certainly we need not think that we must idealize the dead. The truth is that most of us are mixtures of good and evil, strength and weakness. We live together as real persons and not as plaster saints, irritating as well as loving one another. That's the way life is. But without pretending to be what we are not, we should gladly honor the one who has died by remembering his or her life, by celebrating the good in it, and by offering our memories to the God who accepts us in the mixture of good and bad that we all are.

5. To renew community ties among the living

I suppose that almost every community has someone who never got over the shock of bereavement. Perhaps a widow has become a recluse, having shut herself off from the outside world. When her husband died, all the life went out of her also. So she pulled the drapes, took out the telephone, stopped seeing old friends, and just sat inside, to wait out the rest of her years in loneliness and grief.

One of the purposes of funeral rites is to keep that from happening. Friends visiting, sharing memories, joining in ties of worship—these are ways to prevent a person from withdrawing to nurse a grief, encouraging him or her to rejoin the world of the living.

Some years ago I was bothered by the custom of friends bringing food to mourners, or sharing a dinner with them after the funeral. Imagine, partying after the burial! But today that custom looks different to me. It is a way of affirming the life that goes on. It is a way of doing something tangible at a time when most of us feel helpless. It is a way of restoring the ties of human community when some of those ties have just been severed. It is a way of surrounding the grief-stricken with friends, who in effect are saying: "You still have us. And we will not let you be alone."

6. To put death in some kind of religious perspective

It is not merely a casual custom that moves men and women to turn to religion when a death occurs. Deep moments of human life seem to require solemn acts of worship that bind us once again to God.

Death raises deep questions about the meaning of human life. Death makes us wonder what it's all about, what our days add up to. It makes us ask what, if anything, awaits us past the grave. Death forces us to ask what values and causes are worth living for. All these are religious questions. And one of the purposes of funerals is to help people experience death in an overall perspective of trust that God is in charge of the universe, so that in some final sense whatever happens to us is "all right."

Now, I would be misleading you if I gave the impression that everybody who attends a funeral shares such a faith. One of the facts of our time is that increasing numbers of people find it hard to make much sense of traditional religious language, especially the language that gets dusted off sometimes for funerals—language about Judgment Day, the Second Coming of Jesus, heaven and hell, and resurrection. Later in the book I want to discuss changing beliefs about death and life after death. Right now let me just whet your appetite with these words by Rev. Edgar Jackson, a Methodist minister who has for a long time studied grief and funeral customs: "The talk about heaven and hell is as outmoded as the moon of green cheese in an age of astronauts who are prepared to colonize the moon."[15]

Here is our problem as I see it: At death we want to affirm a trust in God, who has both life and death in his keeping. But the ideas and images that we have inherited about life after death sound stranger and stranger to us all the time. We must keep searching for more adequate ways to express our faith.

How can funerals be improved?

We have talked about the main purposes of funeral rites, and have recognized that many persons feel that traditional forms do not fulfill these purposes well enough. Let me make two suggestions about how to create more meaningful rites when death occurs.

First, families need to take a much more active role in planning and participating in the funeral. Instead of having a priest, minister, or rabbi merely read out of a book, the family should help him create the service. They should think about what the person who died meant to them, what memories they want to share publicly, what religious convictions they want the service to express.

This includes their sharing by participation. One family I know of gathered around the kitchen table before going to the funeral home where their father had been taken. They shared their feelings, and said a prayer together that meant more to them than all the public rituals.

When my own son died at the age of two and one half, just our family, a minister-friend, and one other family friend were at the graveside. George's two brothers and two sisters each carried a flower, which they placed on the little casket as part of the service. It meant a lot to us all to be able to have a small role in that brief service.

Here is another example of what I mean by participation. Recently an elder in our church went out of the city to attend the funeral of a longtime friend. This friend was not part of a church, so the minister who conducted the service had never known him. Why have a stranger strain to say something just because he is a minister? My friend, a layman, could much more meaningfully have spoken that day, by sharing what he knew out of long and close acquaintance, as well as out of his own faith.

The more ways we find to involve family and friends in rituals at time of death, the more real they will become to us.

Second, we need to begin to think of alternatives to the traditional form of public visitation, public worship service, and public committal.

One family in our church created a new form that many of their friends found helpful. There was no visitation at all, no display of the body in a casket. On the day of burial, only family and friends went to the graveside for a committal service. Since there were no strangers present, we were able to speak to each other quite personally about what the loss of this good man meant to us all. Then a day later (it was a Sunday afternoon), the entire church family and other friends gathered in the sanctuary for a memorial service. The whole congregation sang, prayed, and affirmed their faith together. The choir sang a stirring anthem. And together we thanked God for our friend's life with us. After the service, we all met the family in Fellowship Hall to express our caring —but without having to make comments about the appearance of the body, as in a visitation. Afterward many people said to me, "That's the way I want it!"

There is no one "right" way to do a funeral. What is

important is that we think together about what a death means to us so that we can share meaningful rites, and not merely endure an empty routine.

We live in a time of changing funeral customs and of shifting beliefs about life after death. It is safe to predict that by the time you have your own family, more changes will have occurred. Now is a good time for you to begin to sift through the various points of view and think about which makes the most sense to you. Perhaps when someone you love dies you will be able to help the church find ways to express its faith in words and forms that are especially fitting for yourself and your day.

A P.S. on not knowing how to act at a funeral

One of my junior high friends wrote me a note that I want to mention at the end of our discussion about funerals. The note told about a funeral, and added: "I was ready to burst out with laughter. I didn't know how to act. I think it was because I had never been to one before. Should I have been embarrassed if I did burst aloud?"

Here is the answer I would give: "You don't need to be embarrassed! You're probably right that the newness of the experience threw you a bit. Also, when we are anxious or unsure of ourselves we sometimes feel like laughing. Another part of your problem is that nobody had told you what was expected of you. It used to be that certain ways of behaving were carefully prescribed for mourners—but not anymore. What it all adds up to is that in the charged emotions of a funeral, a brand-new situation, you didn't know what to do. But you didn't burst out, did you? So don't be afraid of your feelings—you're okay!"

Chapter 5

Chapter 5

Hopes People Live By—
And Die By

Death cannot be discussed without considering various beliefs about life after death. Now it is time to take a closer look at some of them. You have come to a place in your own life when your views may be changing. You are perhaps beginning to question beliefs you were brought up with, as you try to "put it all together" for yourself. In this chapter I do not want to do your thinking for you. I want rather to outline some traditional and modern beliefs so that you can have something to "chew on" as you come to your own understanding of what death means and how to face it.

Some hopes that do not include "life after death"

If we reserve the phrase "life after death" for beliefs in continuing personal existence, it is clear that the hopes by which many people live and die do not include that one.

Many people face the prospect of their own death by some hope in the human future. They believe that they will live on, not as persons, but in their children, in memory and influence, in the triumph of a cause. This kind of belief has been put clearly by Rabbi Grollman:

> Man is immortal: *in body,* through his children; *in thought,* through the survival of his memory; *in influence,* by virtue of the continuance of his personality as a force among those who come after him; and *ideally,* through the identification with the timeless things of the spirit.[16]

A person who has no expectation of personal survival beyond death can adopt an attitude of merely having personal pleasure while he is here—"Live fast, die young, and have a good-looking corpse." But many people who see death as their personal end try to savor life each day and leave the world a little bit better for their being here. An ancient philosopher by the name of Epictetus, who had a deep sense of wanting to be a good steward of the gifts of life, said, "We have to leave the feast of life quietly and gracefully, giving our thanks to God for having invited us to participate in it and to admire his works."[17]

Awhile back, a church group was discussing this subject and thinking about the possibility that perhaps this life is all we have. Perhaps we have no more a life after death than we had a life before birth. One woman was quite disturbed by this thought. She said: "But nothing would have any meaning then! Life isn't always such great stuff, you know!" To her comment another person replied: "Oh, but life would mean so much more. For if we knew this is all we've got, perhaps we'd treasure it, take better care of it, love it and one another more deeply." Such would be the faith of someone who did not believe in personal existence beyond death, but who did believe in living this life to the full in a Christian way.

What were the earliest beliefs in life after death like?

Belief in a personal existence after death is a very, very old idea. Early man of the Upper Paleolithic era (about 30,000 to 10,000 B.C.) buried food, tools, and ornaments with his dead, apparently believing that they would be useful in an afterlife very much like the one on earth. Scholars tell us that all primitive peoples of ancient and modern times have believed that man possesses a soul which lives on in ghostly form after his death. Probably one of the "evidences" for such belief was *dreams*. In their dreams our ancestors "saw" their dead fathers or sisters still "alive," hunting game or pounding grain or even talking to them. You and I regard dreams as our unconscious mind sorting out memories and impressions while we sleep, but to the primitive man they were probably "contacts" with the spirits of the "other world."

What about modern beliefs in spiritualism?

One of the commonest questions raised by young people is, "Can persons who are living communicate with the dead?" To be sure, there are always plenty of persons making such claims, and television shows such as *Night Gallery* keep the rumor going. In England, the Society for Psychical Research examines such claims, though by 1967 no convincing evidence had yet been offered. Experiences of making contact with the dead (when they are not just plain fakery) are probably best understood, like dreams, as the workings of our own minds rather than as real messages from a spirit world.

Let me cite an example. A number of years ago the late Bishop James Pike told about his experiences communicating with his dead son. Much later, the man who was the bishop's personal chaplain said that all the supposed contacts came while Pike was deeply lost in grief over the sudden death of his son, who had committed suicide. The chaplain said that Pike "became a sponge" for anything supernatural, and sought out people (including a medium— someone who purports to be able to contact the dead) who would reinforce his ideas. "How do you reason with someone in acute shock?" asked the chaplain. You remember how we said earlier that the shock of grief can produce many emotional responses. Perhaps experiences like these can better be understood as due to shock and grief rather than the existence of a spirit world. The chaplain spoke out because, he said, "I think the record needs to be set straight so the world will remember that a great man's final bizarre experience was during a time of severe shock."[18]

Once I was called urgently to the hospital by a young woman who was terribly upset. Suddenly, in the prime of life, a dear friend of hers had just died. The girl was sick to her stomach, felt the nearness of the dead woman, as though she could almost hear her speak or reach out and touch her. Now, someone could easily interpret that as the result of the dead woman "trying to get through." Such is the sort of explanation believers in spiritualism give. But a more reasonable explanation, I believe, is that the young woman was in shock, not having had time to let the reality of the death sink in. She was still very angry with God for "taking her" and leaving less worthy women still alive. All these grief feelings were making her sick and producing a strange sense of the nearness of the woman who had died.

What are some of the different kinds of belief in life after death?

One of the ideas commonly held is belief in the *immortality of the soul*. The *soul* is thought to be a part of us that cannot perish, and is released at the death of the body, either for a personal life with God or to be reabsorbed into God or the universe much as a drop of water might fall into the ocean or a spark rejoin a fire. This belief does not come from the Bible, as many believe, but from philosophers of ancient Greece. They believed that man was made up of a mortal body and an immortal soul; that the body was bad or an illusion; and that death was a gain because the soul was released from the prison of the body. In times past, philosophers have tried to locate the soul. One said it was composed of small, fiery atoms in the chest; another that it was found near the brain. Various theories were brought forth about where and how souls originated and were joined by bodies. Today most people who hold this belief would probably think of the soul as the self or personality of a human being, whatever makes him or her an "I." This belief is a way of affirming the ultimate value of persons.

Another widely held belief, especially in lands where Hinduism and Buddhism are influential, is that of *reincarnation*. This is the idea that after death a soul is reborn in another human form, or sometimes even in an animal form. Often this idea is connected with the thought that after a number of existences the soul, which has "worked off" its wrongs and illusions, can finally enter a state of peaceful nonexistence called *Nirvana*.

One of the attractions of the idea of reincarnation is that it "solves" a problem that perplexes other religions—namely, why apparently good and innocent people suffer. This belief says that everyone is getting just what his deeds deserve all the time. For example, if a person is born blind, or crippled, or mentally retarded, he is being punished for misdeeds in an earlier existence. But if he lives well now, he will get his reward by being born better off in the next incarnation. One early church thinker, named Origen, accepted these ideas of reincarnation, but the church rejected them at that time and has continued to do so.

It is interesting to note that around age twelve many persons seem to believe in reincarnation, even if they grow up in religions that reject the idea, such as Judaism and Christianity. Also, reincarnation is similar to early childhood ideas. Many young children believe that when someone dies, a new baby is born.

Other ideas about life after death include judgment, resurrection, heaven and hell. These ideas are part of the Jewish-Christian religious tradition that comes from the Bible. Since in our country this heritage is the strongest religious influence, I want to discuss it a bit more thoroughly than I have described some of the other beliefs. For whether or not you believe them, these ideas are a part of the cultural air you breathe.

What does the Bible say about life after death?

If I told you that the Bible gives one clear answer to this question, I would be misleading you. The truth is that the Bible gives many different answers. Sometimes they are complicated, and do not all fit neatly together. The reason is that the books of the Bible were written over a period of at least eleven hundred years. Imagine that today you were writing the last chapter in a book someone else began in the year 800. Think of what a fantastic range of ideas that book might cover: from belief in demons and witches to manned space flight, from the divine right of kings to representative democracy, from the burning of unbelievers to the world-embracing love of Pope John XXIII. That is the way it is with the Bible: its pages reveal many different beliefs about God and the world, some of which will sound quite strange to any modern person.

Let us try to get a sense of the whole Bible message by dividing its view of life after death into three parts: (1) the old Hebrew view, (2) the developed Jewish view, and (3) the early Christian view. The going may be a little rough, but if you stick with it, you will have a better idea of where today's beliefs have come from.

1. What was the old Hebrew view about life after death?

This may be a surprise to you, but the oldest books of the Bible, which deal with the times of Abraham and Moses, David and Solomon, Amos, Hosea, and Jeremiah, do not show any belief in life after death at all—no judgment, no heaven, no hell. It was not until very late in the Old Testament period that such an idea came into Jewish faith.

The reason was that the Hebrew people had an intense sense of God being with them *here*—in human society and history. So their hope was for long life and many children as part of a "chosen people" dwelling securely in a good land. In the story of God meeting Abraham, the promise is not that he will be immortal, but that he will be the father of a great nation. The Hebrews' hope was for a good future here on earth.

The Hebrews did not believe, though, that people were entirely "extinguished" at death. They believed that beneath the earth was a place called Sheol (which the Greeks called Hades), to which all souls of the dead went to exist as drab, dark, weak, and hopeless spirits. We cannot call that an idea of life after death because there was really no *life* to it— these shadows were cut off from God, without joy or hope. All people went there, good and bad alike, and there were no rewards or punishments. Sheol was not a fate to be desired! The idea of Sheol really underlines the Hebrew belief that real life is life in this world, and that the tragedy of death was that a person dropped out of history in which God was working with his people.

How did this view begin to change—and why?

As long as Israel survived and prospered as a nation, the people could put their hope in its future. But Israel ran into rough times: it got caught in international warfare with the great empires of Babylonia, Assyria, Egypt, Persia, and Greece. About six hundred years before Christ, Israel was invaded and destroyed, and the "cream of the crop" were sent into foreign lands as exiles.

This began to raise some new questions for the people. Now that they could not pin their hopes on the nation's future, they began to wonder more about their own future. Also, when the going was toughest, the prophets held out hope that someday God would intervene to vindicate Israel, judge her enemies, and reestablish a righteous people to dwell in peace and prosperity in the Promised Land. As time went by, the people began to wonder if God might not raise up the righteous dead to have a share in that Great Day. They had always believed that God rewarded the righteous and punished the wicked—in this life. But they began to see that life does not work out so neatly—sometimes the good people suffered while the bad people were prosperous. Maybe, they thought, God will show *beyond* death the justice he did not give *before* death. It did not seem fair that those who obeyed God should simply die without any hope. Sheol began to seem too good a place for the wicked and not good enough for the righteous. So, by the time of The Book of Daniel, written during a period of intense persecution a century and a half before Christ, we find a clear belief that at a Day of Judgment, God would raise up the dead, some to everlasting life and some to eternal contempt.

2. What was the form of the developed Jewish hope?

Here is the startling thing about that belief: the Jews did not believe that a good man's soul went to heaven, but that on Judgment Day his whole body would be brought back to life here on earth. This is called belief in the *resurrection of the body*. The Jews did not believe that human beings have an immortal soul that is imperishable. They believed that when a man died he really died—all of him. Their hope was that on Judgment Day, when God triumphed over Israel's enemies and established on earth his rule of justice and peace, he would by a new creation restore the dead to life —total life, body and soul, here in a transformed world. Still the hope was social and worldly—not hope for a "spiritual" life in another world, but hope for an age of peace, justice, and love in this world. The reason for resurrection was to give people a share in the new world where they would live according to God's intention for all people:

The wolf shall lie down with the lamb. . . . They shall
not hurt or destroy in all my holy mountain. . . . They
shall beat their swords into plowshares and their
spears into pruning hooks: nation shall not lift up
sword against nation, neither shall they learn war any
more. . . . Then shall the eyes of the blind be opened,
the ears of the deaf unstopped . . . and the earth shall
be full of the knowledge of God, as the waters cover
the sea.[19]

Did all the Jewish people have the same ideas about the resurrection?

No. In the time of Jesus, the air was full of different
speculations about the *end times.* A group called *Pharisees*
believed in angels, spirits, and resurrection, while *Sad-
ducees* rejected such ideas. Many people were expecting
the world as they knew it to come to an end soon, and for
God (or his appointed agent, called the Messiah) to come to
inaugurate the New Age. Many people were greatly em-
broidering the ideas of Paradise, Satan, and Gehenna. Perhaps it would be well to attempt to define what these terms
meant.

Paradise was a word and an idea that the Jews adapted
from the Persians (who had conquered them several centu-
ries earlier); it referred to a beautiful garden where the righteous were believed to go after death—a kind of renewed
Garden of Eden. *Satan* had also developed under Persian
influence. When the Jewish people were suffering terribly,
and did not want to blame God for the evil in the world, they
developed the idea that temporarily this world was under
the rule of an evil power (Satan or the devil) whom God
would overthrow on the Day of Judgment. Have you ever

wondered why we picture Satan as we do? In the book of Revelation he reminds us of great sea dragons that appear in Old Testament legends. Probably he drew some features from a satyr or wild goat called Azazel, from ancient times. Sometimes he was thought of as an angel who led a rebellion against God and so was cast out of heaven. So all those ideas add up to a Satan who has the shining body and wings of an angel, the forked tail of a dragon, and the horns, ears, and feet of a satyr. Of course, many people do not believe that a Satan exists: he is a symbol of evil. As for *Gehenna,* it was a "hell" named after the smoldering garbage pit of Jerusalem; hence the association of hell with undying worms and unquenchable fires. In the Middle Ages the church also developed the idea of *purgatory,* where people not good enough for heaven or bad enough for hell worked off their sins in preparation for heaven. Imaginations ran wild in devising torments suitable for various categories of sinners! Also, a place called *limbo* was invented where unbaptized babies and righteous pagans were kept, without suffering but excluded from the vision of God. Men have usually painted more vivid pictures of hell than of heaven (except maybe for Muhammad, who equipped heaven with couches, fragrant fruits, and dancing girls!).

There was no consistent picture of what the last days would be like. Sometimes people pictured Paradise and Gehenna as appearing together on earth at the Last Day, sometimes as existing side by side in a heaven. Many very fanciful ideas were "in the air" in Jesus' day.

What did Jesus himself believe?

We cannot be sure just what Jesus himself believed. We know that he shared many of the beliefs of the time: he believed that the end of the present age was coming, and that how men responded to him would influence their fate then; he believed apparently in judgment and resurrection and angels (with the Pharisees); he refused, though, to speculate about the end or "set the date." Jesus had very little to say about all the popular imaginings of what the Age to Come would be like.

In one way he was very different from most people of his time. Jesus taught that the *Kingdom of God* is not just a new kind of life that will come at the end, but that it is also already in the world for those who will accept it. He taught that *the Kingdom of Heaven is in the midst of you*—here and now. The rule of God could be known not only when history drew to a close, but now—wherever the poor heard good news, the sick were made whole, guilty people were forgiven, the imprisoned were set free, and enemies were reconciled to one another. Wherever peace and love and justice and healing came alive, there the New Age had already dawned. For this reason the writer of the Gospel of John said that anyone who knows God and Christ already has eternal life. Jesus clearly believed that in some future, God was going to "renovate" the earth. But he also believed that heaven became real right here and now whenever people fulfilled God's purpose to make a human family of peace and love.

3. *What did the early Christian church believe?*

In general, the first Christians accepted the beliefs they had inherited from the Pharisees. There was one big difference. They believed that Jesus was the Messiah, and that he would come back someday to usher in Judgment Day and the resurrection of the dead. They believed that, after being crucified, Jesus himself had been resurrected—a kind of stamp of approval by God upon his ministry, and a sign that the New Age whose fulfillment was still to come had already dawned. Most early Christians believed that Jesus was coming back very soon. In the New Testament we find the idea that the world as we know it would end, that those still living and the Christian dead would all together be caught up to meet Jesus in the sky, and that they would live together in a re-created world. Here again you see that the hope was not so much for another world (a heaven) as for a new world (a heaven on earth). When Jesus did not return, Christians began to change their timetable of hope, especially by using the idea that "with the Lord a thousand years is but a day." In our own time some groups still expect the Second Coming of Jesus very soon, while other Christians take the idea to be a symbol that finally God's purpose will be fulfilled in all the world.

When Jesus did not return, that caused a special problem for the early Christians. At first they had believed that Christians who died would not have to wait long before they were resurrected at Judgment Day. But when his coming was delayed, they began to wonder what would happen to dead believers in the meantime. So they developed the idea that, right when they died, Christians were *with the Lord* in spirit, though they would have to wait for Judgment Day to be reclothed in the resurrection body (a transformed, "spiritual" body). Perhaps the finest expression of the trust Christians had comes from the apostle Paul, who wrote: "If we live, we live to the Lord; if we die, we die to the Lord; so whether we live or whether we die, we are the Lord's."[20]

What do modern-day Christians believe about life after death?

That all depends upon *which* modern-day Christians you are talking about, because there is great variety in the beliefs people hold today. About ten years ago two sociologists studied members of various Christian groups. Complete belief in life after death was expressed by 49 percent of Methodists, 64 percent of Presbyterians, 72 percent of American Baptists, 75 percent of Catholics, and 97 percent of Southern Baptists.[21] So you can see that there are wide differences between groups.

There are also varieties of belief *within* churches. One Sunday morning we took a survey in our church of four hundred members who had come together for worship. About 84 percent expressed belief in the "immortality of the soul," though 38 percent believed that we live on only "through memory and influence." Just about half of the congregation expressed belief in such traditional ideas as resurrection of the dead, judgment beyond death, and the Second Coming of Christ. Three fourths of the church denied that salvation is possible only for Christians, and 70 percent denied belief in heaven and hell or had "no opinion." Fifty-four percent agreed that their ideas on the subject are "very confused," and 81 percent said that "it is time for a thorough rethinking" of Christian beliefs about life after death.

On another Sunday morning not long ago, I gave everyone in church pencils and paper, and asked each to write briefly on "What I Personally Think and Feel About Life After Death." I would like to share just a few of these responses. I think you will be interested in the variety of opinions expressed by these Christians of today.

1. I would hope there is some sort of continuation of existence after death—though it doesn't seem too likely. Mostly I trust God's plan—for life and death, whatever it may be—and know that it is good.

2. I do not believe in life after death, but that your way of life on earth helps guide those you left behind and in this way your life is complete.

3. This is something I've given much thought to—with no certain results! It seems impossible that everything just *stops* for one at death, but how "life" can exist escapes me! Perhaps it is just wishful thinking to hope for any "life after death." Sometimes the Indian, etc., ideas of reincarnation appeal to me!

4. I feel we are no more equipped to have insight into life after death than the embryo is to have insight into life after birth.

5. I believe the soul is released upon death of the body—all souls rejoin the Creator at that time. One makes and lives in his own heaven or hell while alive on earth.

6. I believe that we would not have been created so wonderfully into this world to just die and return to dust and expect to live on in someone's memory. I believe God in his greatness has prepared something much better—beyond our comprehension.

7. God has created a very special world wherein lies order. To say that I know what comes after this life is absurd. I do trust in his plan—I feel that the thing which makes a person unique—himself—call it soul, personality, spirit, etc., goes on in a special way. Knowing there is a physical end to this precious thing we call life makes this gift (life) a day-to-day thanksgiving.

8. I don't believe in life after death. If we do have souls, I am undecided as to where they go. I do believe that men in dying decay and thus become a chemical part of the life to follow.

9. If we are truly Christians, we must accept the message of Christ—all of his teachings—and he did emphasize the life after death and his return. I am confused at times by the immensity of God's universe and certain scientific discoveries in relation to it.

10. It was comforting as a child to know that those I had loved would not be lost to me forever, that I would see and be with them in heaven. I now no longer believe in heaven as the same place I thought of as a child, but if we can't believe in a heaven, what's our religion all about?

11. I believe that at least one important dimension of salvation is for the living and the present. I do not know whether there is life after death, but I have faith that if there is, God will treat me and all mankind with the same justice with which I have received love and

mercy at his hands in the present. My past, present, and future are in his hands.

12. I'll wait and see. It'll be an adventure—(I hope).

Why so much questioning of beliefs these days?

I suppose that "once upon a time" beliefs in Christ's Second Coming, Judgment Day, heaven and hell were much more clearly fixed and firmly believed than they are today. The main reason is that for the past several hundred years, largely under the influence of science, we have been revising our way of looking at our world.

In days past, believers could think of heaven as "up there" somewhere, but in a time of men walking on the moon, Pioneer 10 streaking toward Jupiter and beyond, and radio telescopes that measure our universe in terms of millions of light-years, it is hard to make sense of the old language. Likewise, the discovery of evolution makes us think of man not as a fallen being (who was sentenced to the fate of death as punishment) but as a developing creature whose future lies before him. Death is to us a part of the natural cycle of life—not a punishment for Adam's sin in the Garden of Eden. And we have also come to a time when not many of us are willing to accept religious beliefs just because a supposed authority—whether Bible or church—tells us it is so. We think of religion as an expression of the deepest truths of our own life experience—and we do not "experience" life beyond death.

At the same time as we have changed our way of looking at the universe, we have come to a new sense of responsibility for our earth. Earth rather than heaven has become the focus of our hopes and strivings.

I vividly remember an evening back in 1963 which I spent in the home of an elderly black lady in Mississippi. I was there to help register Negro voters, who until that time had been denied the right to vote as free citizens. This lady had been a servant to a governor of that state, had suffered much indignity, had very little of the good things of life—but through all her poverty and oppression kept alive a radiant spirit of faith and hope. As I left her home I turned to a friend and said, "There has got to be a heaven for people like her!" I was feeling like those ancient Jews who thought it just was not fair for good people to die without hope of justice. I do not know whether I really believed in heaven then or not. But I do know that I am more and more ready to say that achieving justice, freedom, safety, health, and plenty are our human responsibilities to one another in this world—and we cannot shove those tasks off on God to take care of in a hereafter.

A Roman Catholic leader in Brazil, Dom Helder Câmara, who is deeply concerned for justice there, has said it like this:

> In my country there are areas that you would flatter by calling them under-developed: there men live as in the days of cavemen, and they are happy to eat what they find in garbage heaps. So what do I tell these people? To put up with it for the sake of the next life? Eternity starts here on earth, not in heaven.[22]

Now that we have all seen the planet earth from the depths of space, spinning its way as a beautiful blue and green oasis of life against the black of space, we may hope for a new sense that we are all brothers and sisters, and responsible together for the wise care of the world and the people whom God has given us.

What, then, does the Biblical story have to say to us?

I am sure that as you read about Biblical beliefs, you find some of them strange and hard to understand. That is because we look at the world very differently from the way people did thousands of years ago. Yet we also have much in common with them. The Biblical images of the future world are *symbols*—that means, pictures of realities that we cannot speak about in cold prose. Many of the deepest human intuitions cannot be spoken—that is why we need poets, artists, dramatists, and prophets. You and I do not have to take the Biblical symbols literally. But I believe that we should listen to them carefully and take them seriously.

Think about the Biblical symbols of the New Age for a moment. Surely you noticed that they are not merely self-centered, as though the big issue is that you and I should live forever. Rather, the Bible pictures a new world, a New Jerusalem, a Kingdom of God—all of which is to say a new human society in which love and peace and justice are made real. Jesus drew a picture of Judgment Day, and said that the test of a person's worthiness will be whether he fed the hungry, clothed the naked, visited the sick and imprisoned, welcomed the stranger.

We need visions like those, for human life is measured by the quality of our dreams. Of course, life and death are mysteries beyond our full comprehension. But these Biblical images, I believe, give us an agenda for our living and a hope for our dying. They invite us, in the midst of a world full of hurts and hatreds, to live as parables of what the world will be like when God refashions it as his Kingdom. We are here to share God's love for all that he has made. We are here to help bind up wounds, to help usher in a day when the whole human family may live together in peace and unity. That is quite an agenda for any human life.

When we die, most likely we and our world will still represent unfinished business. These hopes are not apt to be fulfilled in our lifetime. Yet they are goals worth living and dying for. And when death overtakes us, it is hoped we will be able in trust to return both our lives and our world to the God who gave them. And to believe, in the words of the song, that "He's got the whole world in his hands!"

Notes

1. Simon Yudkin, "Death and the Young," in Arnold Toynbee *et al., Man's Concern with Death* (McGraw-Hill Book Co., Inc., 1968), pp. 46–55.
2. *The Saturday Evening Post,* Nov. 19, 1961.
3. Elisabeth Kübler-Ross, *On Death and Dying* (The Macmillan Company, 1969).
4. Dr. Walter Alvarez, quoted in W. Kitay, "Let's Restore the Dignity of Dying," reprinted from *Today's Health* in a now-defunct digest for ministers, the name of which I cannot recall.
5. Thomas Powers, "Learning to Die," *Harper's Magazine,* June 1971, pp. 72 ff.; and Glenn Vernon, *Sociology of Death* (The Ronald Press Company, 1970), pp. 14–15.
6. Herbert Zim and Sonia Bleeker, *Life and Death* (William Morrow & Company, Inc., 1970), p. 23.
7. *Ibid.,* p. 21.
8. Charles Kemp, *Physicians of the Soul* (The Macmillan Company, 1947), pp. 111–112.
9. The five kinds of childhood grief feelings are discussed in Earl Grollman (ed.), *Explaining Death to Children* (Beacon Press, Inc., 1970), pp. 3–27.

10. Sylvia Anthony, *The Child's Discovery of Death* (Harcourt, Brace and Company, Inc., 1940), p. 151.

11. Marjorie E. Mitchell, *The Child's Attitude Towards Death* (Schocken Books, Inc., 1967), p. 107.

12. Edwin Shneidman, "You and Death," in *Psychology Today,* June 1971.

13. Grollman (ed.), *op. cit.,* p. 14.

14. Shneidman, *loc. cit.*

15. Edgar Jackson, "The Theological, Psychological, and Philosophical Dimensions of Death in Protestantism," in Grollman (ed.), *op. cit.,* pp. 171–195.

16. Earl Grollman, "The Ritualistic and Theological Approach of the Jew," in Grollman (ed.), *op. cit.,* p. 231.

17. Jacques Choron, *Death and Western Thought* (Collier Books, 1963), p. 72.

18. Lester Kinsolving, *San Francisco Sunday Examiner and Chronicle,* July 25, 1971.

19. Isa. 11:6, 9; 2:4; 11:9.

20. Rom. 14:8.

21. Jeffrey K. Hadden, *The Gathering Storm in the Churches* (Doubleday & Company, Inc., 1969), p. 58.

22. Dom Helder Câmara, in *Concern,* May 1972.